AF270625

Basset Hounds

by Julie Murray

abdobooks.com

Published by Abdo Kids, a division of ABDO, P.O. Box 398166, Minneapolis, Minnesota 55439.
Copyright © 2024 by Abdo Consulting Group, Inc. International copyrights reserved in all countries.
No part of this book may be reproduced in any form without written permission from the publisher.
Abdo Kids Jumbo™ is a trademark and logo of Abdo Kids.

Printed in the United States of America, North Mankato, Minnesota.

102023

012024

Photo Credits: Alamy, Getty Images, Shutterstock, Thinkstock

Production Contributors: Teddy Borth, Jennie Forsberg, Grace Hansen
Design Contributors: Candice Keimig, Pakou Moua

Library of Congress Control Number: 2023937674

Publisher's Cataloging-in-Publication Data

Names: Murray, Julie, author.

Title: Basset hounds / by Julie Murray

Description: Minneapolis, Minnesota : Abdo Kids, 2024 | Series: Dogs | Includes online resources and
    index.

Identifiers: ISBN 9781098268497 (lib. bdg.) | ISBN 9781098269197 (ebook) | ISBN 9781098269548
    (Read-to-Me ebook)

Subjects: LCSH: Basset hound--Juvenile literature. | Hounds--Juvenile literature. | Dogs--Juvenile
    literature. | Dogs--Behavior--Juvenile literature. | Animal behavior--Juvenile literature.

Classification: DDC 599.772--dc23

Table of Contents

Basset Hounds

Basset hounds are known for their droopy eyes and relaxed personalities. They are also one of the best scent dogs!

Basset hounds **originated** in

France hundreds of years ago.

They were **bred** to track and hunt

small game, such as rabbits.

Europe
France
Africa
N
S
E
W
7

Basset hounds have great

stamina. They can track a scent

for miles without stopping.

Basset hounds have short legs, long bodies, and large heads. They stand about 15 inches (38.1 cm) tall at the shoulders. They can weigh up to 65 pounds (29.5 kg).

Basset hounds have smooth, short coats. Their coats can be different colors. Most have white-tipped tails. The dogs can be easily spotted in fields as they hunt.

Basset hounds have long ears, droopy eyes, and hanging lips. This gives them a sad look that is hard to resist!

Grooming

Basset hounds need weekly brushing and an occasional bath. Ear **infections** are common, so cleaning the ears is important.

Exercise

Basset hounds should have daily walks. This helps prevent weight gain. Basset hounds are happy to relax, but also enjoy all the scents of the outdoors.

Personality

Basset hounds are easygoing dogs. They do well with families and other pets. They can be hard to train. Basset hounds will follow a scent wherever it leads. A leash or fenced yard is needed.

More Facts

- Basset hounds can be loud. They bark, howl, and **bay**. They tend to howl when left alone for long periods of time.

- Their long ears sweep and stir up scents on the ground. Their loose mouth skin traps a scent and keeps it close to their nose.

- The American Kennel Club officially recognized the Basset Hound in 1885.

Glossary

bay – to bark with long, deep tones.

bred – developed over time for a certain purpose.

infection – an illness caused by germs.

originated – came from or began in a particular place or situation.

stamina – the strength to handle long effort or disappointment.

Index

Visit **abdokids.com** to access crafts, games, videos, and more!